# Table of Contents

# Detailed Contents

# Introduction

 The role of this workbook is to provide you with the tools to forecast the financial operations of your business. This workbook focuses on helping you forecast the cash needs of your business, with an emphasis on the cash requirements during the critical startup phase and initial months of operations. It includes sections on:

- Startup expenses
- Sales and revenue
- Monthly operating and other expenses
- Determining your startup and operating cash needs

We've designed the workbook to be a companion to *Finance Without Fear: A Guide to Creating and Managing a Profitable Business*. If you haven't read *Finance Without Fear*, you might want to do so in conjunction with using the tools in this workbook.

It's also designed to be used in conjunction with the Business Forecasting Model that's available through our website at www.FinanceWithoutFear.com. You'll find instructions for accessing this model in the workbook's Appendix.

Structured to be used as a hands-on business forecasting tool, the workbook is divided into six sections. The key elements necessary to successfully forecast the financial operation of your business are described first, then you'll have an opportunity to conduct some research and make notes about the estimates for your business, and finally you'll use the Business Forecasting Model to develop financial projections.

Specifically, *Section 1* focuses on the planning of your business. In this section, you'll have the opportunity to think through your reasons for starting the business, the products or services you'll offer, and how you expect your business to compare to the industry and your competitors.

*Section 2* is devoted to projecting your startup expenses. In this section, we'll guide you through the identification and estimation of the startup expenses of your business.

In *Section 3*, we'll help you estimate the pricing, cost of goods sold and sales volume for your products or services.

*Section 4* is devoted to the estimation of the monthly operating expenses and well as to the estimation of any payments you must make to your lenders or owners.

*Section 5* focuses on using the information from the earlier sections to develop cash flow projections and to determine the startup cash needs of your business.

*Section 6* is dedicated to analyzing the sensitivity of your key assumptions and estimates.

Note that although the printed tables in this workbook are taken from the spreadsheet model, to get the most out of this workbook and the Business Forecasting Model, you should download the model and work through it as you read the sections in the workbook.

Let's begin by reviewing some of the material you'll need to forecast the cash flows and financial statements for your business.

# Planning Your Business

 If you want to create a profitable business, your first step should be to make a plan. In this section, we'll discuss the various steps involved in planning your business. These include defining your purpose, choosing the products and services you'll offer, selecting your operating strategies, identifying your sources of competitive advantage, and determining how the key financial indicators will stack up to the competition.

## The Purpose of Your Business

There are many types of products and services a business can offer. Different types of businesses and products carry varying levels of risk and profit. They may also require different types of skills and expertise.

If you're thinking of starting a business, one of the most important first steps is to do a self-assessment of your goals for the business, your strengths and weaknesses, how you want to spend your day, and why you're passionate about starting this particular business.

### Goals for the Business

If you're going to form a business, it's very important that you understand why you're doing so and identify your goals for the venture. These goals can include the fulfillment of a long-standing desire to be self-employed, to earn a living without going into an office or factory each day, to be in control of your own financial and professional destiny, to bring a new product or service to the world, or even to make a lot of money. A good way to start is by listing your goals for the business.

**Goals for the Business**

1. _____

2. _____

3. _____

4. _____

5. _____

## Strengths and Weaknesses

If you're going to create your own business, it's essential that you understand your strengths and weaknesses. As we discussed in Chapter 1 of *Finance Without Fear*, businesses make money using either a customer-centric strategy or an operational-centric strategy. It's very difficult for a business to have both an operational-centric and customer-centric focus. A business can be strong in only one of these areas.

It's the same when analyzing your strengths and weaknesses. Your strength may be in sales and marketing or managing or operating the business. Or maybe your strength is in designing products or working to serve the needs of customers. Chances are, you won't be good at all these things, and, in fact, you might not even have a desire to perform some of these tasks. As a business owner, you want to use your strengths to help the business, and hire staff and other professionals to help you in the areas where you are weak.

List your strengths and weaknesses below, and remember to be honest:

| Strengths | Weaknesses |
|---|---|
| _____ | _____ |
| _____ | _____ |
| _____ | _____ |
| _____ | _____ |
| _____ | _____ |

## How Do You Want to Spend Your Day?

To many people, having your own business means you're free—free to work 12-hour days, to work nights and weekends, and to deal with everything from signing million-dollar contracts to making sure the trash gets put out.

As a business owner, you're at liberty to decide how you spend your day. You can wait on customers, market the business, manage operations, or design new products behind a closed office door.

Of course, you don't have to limit yourself to a single activity. You may need or want to spend your day performing a variety of activities. You can spend part of the day marketing the business or dealing with customers, and another part designing new products.

As a business owner, you should recognize that you can't be good at everything and that you should focus your time and energy on the things that you are good at, and hire staff or partner with others in those areas in which your skills are weaker.

Note how you want to spend your day:

---

**How Do You Want to Spend Your Day?**

_____

_____

_____

_____

_____

---

## What Are You Passionate About?

If you're going to form a business and spend a significant part of your time building it, you should choose something you're passionate about. If you're not passionate about the business, you may find it difficult to build it. You may end up viewing it as just another job, and you may find that it's less rewarding than the job you just left.

To be successful, you should be passionate about your business, so think about why this business is important to you. Why you find this business exciting, and why you're willing to work to make it a success.

List why you're passionate about this business:

*Why Are You Passionate About This Business?*

_____

_____

_____

_____

_____

# The Products and Services You Plan to Sell

As you plan your business, it's very important that you consider what products or services you'll offer. This seems like an easy decision, but choosing the right products and services helps define the structure and strategy of the business.

Once you decide on the products and services you'll sell, you'll need to determine the prices you expect to be able to obtain for these products or services.

Use the "Products and Services" worksheet below to list the products or services you plan to sell and the prices you expect to charge.

*Products and Services*

| | Product or Service | Expected Price |
|---|---|---|
| 1. | _____ | _____ |
| 2. | _____ | _____ |
| 3. | _____ | _____ |
| 4. | _____ | _____ |
| 5. | _____ | _____ |
| 6. | _____ | _____ |
| 7. | _____ | _____ |
| 8. | _____ | _____ |
| 9. | _____ | _____ |
| 10. | _____ | _____ |

It's also imperative that you understand who your competitors are and the prices they're charging for their products and services. You should conduct some market research to understand who your competitors are, and if what they charge for their products or services are the same as those you plan to sell. This will help you determine if your pricing expectations are realistic.

Use the "Competitors' Products and Services" worksheet below to list your chief competitors and their prices.

---

### *Competitors' Products and Services*

| Competitor | Competitors'<br>Products or Services | Competitors'<br>Prices |
|---|---|---|
| 1. _____ | _____ | _____ |
| 2. _____ | _____ | _____ |
| 3. _____ | _____ | _____ |
| 4. _____ | _____ | _____ |
| 5. _____ | _____ | _____ |
| 6. _____ | _____ | _____ |
| 7. _____ | _____ | _____ |
| 8. _____ | _____ | _____ |
| 9. _____ | _____ | _____ |
| 10. _____ | _____ | _____ |

---

# Your Strategies

You should also look at the operating strategies used by your competitors, and ask yourself some questions:

- *Are your competitors offering exceptional customer service?* If not, using a customer service strategy might be an effective way to compete.
- *Are your competitors focused on sales and marketing?* If not, you have an opportunity to use sales and marketing as a business strategy.

- *Are your competitors designing and developing innovative products?* If not, you may have an opportunity to compete using an innovation and design strategy.

- *Are your competitors pursuing an operational-centric strategy and trying to be as operationally efficient as possible?* If not, you have an opportunity to increase your profits by producing products and delivering them to customers at a lower cost than your competitors.

List strategies used by competitors:

### Strategies Used by Competitors

_____

_____

_____

_____

_____

_____

List strategies to be used in your own business:

### Strategies to be Used in Your Own Business

_____

_____

_____

_____

_____

_____

# Your Suppliers

If you plan on operating a retail store or manufacturing business, you'll need to research and find the suppliers from whom you'll buy raw materials to be used in your production process or the finished inventory you'll sell in your store.

In reviewing the products offered by different suppliers, it's important to identify any variances in the quality or features of the raw materials and inventory that might affect the value of your products. It's also important to know how much it will cost to purchase the raw materials or inventory.

Finally, it's essential that you know the terms under which suppliers will sell to your business. When you have to pay your suppliers is an important consideration when projecting the cash flow of your business. Some suppliers may give you 30 days to pay; others may allow you 90 days. Since you're a new business, some suppliers may require that you pay cash upon delivery until your business demonstrates that it's making a profit and can pay its bills.

As you research this information, you can use the "Sources of Raw Materials" and "Sources of Inventory" worksheets (see page 7 and 8) to record your notes and compare suppliers.

## Sources of Raw Material

| | Raw Material | Supplier | Price | Payment Terms | Quality Notes |
|---|---|---|---|---|---|
| 1. | | | | | |
| 2. | | | | | |
| 3. | | | | | |
| 4. | | | | | |
| 5. | | | | | |
| 6. | | | | | |
| 7. | | | | | |
| 8. | | | | | |
| 9. | | | | | |
| 10. | | | | | |

*Sources of Inventory*

| | Product | Supplier | Price | Payment Terms | Quality Notes |
|---|---|---|---|---|---|
| 1. | _____ | _____ | _____ | _____ | _____ |
| 2. | _____ | _____ | _____ | _____ | _____ |
| 3. | _____ | _____ | _____ | _____ | _____ |
| 4. | _____ | _____ | _____ | _____ | _____ |
| 5. | _____ | _____ | _____ | _____ | _____ |
| 6. | _____ | _____ | _____ | _____ | _____ |
| 7. | _____ | _____ | _____ | _____ | _____ |
| 8. | _____ | _____ | _____ | _____ | _____ |
| 9. | _____ | _____ | _____ | _____ | _____ |
| 10. | _____ | _____ | _____ | _____ | _____ |

# Your Margins

When planning your startup venture, it's very important that you research the typical margins for your products and services and define the margins you expect to earn from your business.

As we discussed in Chapter 10 of *Finance Without Fear*, a business that uses a customer-centric strategy will need to earn high gross margins to support the additional operating expenses associated with serving its customers.

If you're planning to use a customer-centric strategy and won't earn high gross margins, you should reconsider your business strategy, as you most likely will not be profitable after paying the higher operating expenses.

Likewise, if you're planning to use an operational-centric strategy but don't expect to generate a sufficient sales volume, you may find that your business is unable to cover operating expenses or earn a profit.

Chapter 10 in *Finance Without Fear* presented many examples of the gross, operating and net margins typical for many different types of businesses, and it provided sources of publicly available information on margins. There's also information available on margins by industry on our website www.Finance-WithoutFear.com.

We can't stress enough the importance of researching typical margins for your product or service. You'll need to understand how much you can expect to earn on each sale, the operating expenses that are typical for your industry, and how much profit you expect the business to earn. This information is necessary in order to develop financial projections and will also help you explain to your lenders and investors how your business makes money.

Do some research and then complete the "Margin Comparison" worksheet below with the margins you expect for your business. Be sure you're able to explain the reasons for any significant deviation from industry norms.

| Margin Comparison | My Business | Typical for Industry | Reasons for Any Differences |
|---|---|---|---|
| Gross Margin | | | |
| Operating Margin | | | |
| Net Margin | | | |

# Your Cash Conversion Cycle

As you know from reading *Finance Without Fear*, cash flow is the lifeblood of a business. If a business doesn't have sufficient cash to pay its bills, the business won't survive.

In planning the cash requirements for your business, it's very important that you understand how fast you'll be paid and how quickly you'll be expected to pay your bills. Once you have this information, you can estimate your cash conversion cycle. The components of the cash conversion cycle are described in Chapter 11 of *Finance Without Fear*. This chapter also describes some comparative industry information on cash conversion cycles.

The first component of the cash conversion cycle is the collection period, which measures the number of days it takes for customers to pay for the goods and services they purchase from a business. In other words, when you make a sale, how quickly does the business get the cash?

Use the "Cash Conversion Cycle Comparison" worksheet on page 10 to estimate the collection period for each of the products or services your business expects to sell. Also, estimate how this collection period compares to the industry and note why your business might be different.

The second component of the cash conversion cycle is the payment period, which measures the number of days it takes the business to pay its bills. When your business purchases raw materials or inventory or services from another company, how quickly must it pay for these items?

Again, use the "Cash Conversion Cycle Comparison" worksheet below to estimate the payment period for each of the products and services your business will be purchasing from others. Also, estimate how this payment period compares to the industry and note why your business might be different.

The final component of the cash conversion cycle is the number of days products stay in inventory before they're sold. When your company purchases inventory or manufactures products, how long do these products sit on the shelves before they are sold? A business uses cash to purchase inventory, so having lots of inventory means a business will need more cash.

On the "Cash Conversion Cycle Comparison" worksheet, estimate the number of days of inventory you expect your business to have, how this compares to the industry, and why your business might be different.

Once you've entered the collection period, payment period, and days in inventory estimates for your business and industry, be sure to calculate the cash conversion cycle. Use the formula listed at the bottom of the "Cash Conversion Cycle Comparison" worksheet.

---

### Cash Conversion Cycle Comparison

| | My Business | Typical for Industry | Reasons for Any Differences |
|---|---|---|---|
| Collection Period | _____ | _____ | _____ |
| Payment Period | _____ | _____ | _____ |
| Days in Inventory | _____ | _____ | _____ |
| Cash Conversion Cycle | _____ | _____ | _____ |

*\* Cash Conversion Cycle = Collection Period – Payment Period + Days in Inventory*

---

You should make a particular note of how your cash conversion cycle compares to your industry and your main competitors. If your cash conversion cycle is worse than your competitors', you'll need more cash to run your business, which may put you at a competitive disadvantage. However, if your cash conversion cycle is better than your competitors', you may have a competitive advantage.

Now that you've done the research on your products and services and the costs of providing them, it's time to begin projecting the cash flows and financial statements for your business. In the next section, we discuss your business's startup expenses.

# Startup Expenses

Businesses have three different types of startup expenses:

- The purchase of assets that will be used in the production or sales processes of the business
- The initial purchases of inventory and raw materials
- The out-of-pocket expenses of starting the business

As you plan your business, it's important you consider how much money you'll need for each of these expenses.

## Asset Purchases

Startup asset purchases include the buildings, vehicles, manufacturing equipment, computers, printers, software, cash registers, office equipment and furniture the business purchases to get set up to begin operations.

Probably the most common type of asset acquired for a business is the purchase of equipment. Equipment could include the type used in manufacturing businesses, where the operation is dependent on the use of specialized machinery, such as lathes, bending machines and robots. It might also include the type of equipment used in construction businesses, such as a backhoe or bobcat.

But even service and retail businesses may need to purchase assets. A retail business may need to purchase the tables and racks on which to display its merchandise. A restaurant may need to outfit the kitchen with pots, pans and ovens, and furnish the eating area with tables, chairs, linens and silverware. Even the most basic consulting business relies on the use of a computer and printer.

All these items are examples of assets that a business may need to purchase. Rather than being consumed in the production process, this equipment is intended to last the business for many years.

Use the "Asset Purchases" worksheet below to note your estimated startup expenses. When forecasting the cash flows for these asset purchases, be sure to record the payments at the time the cash is spent. If the business pays the full price at purchase, this should be recorded in the worksheet. If the business is using an installment method, only the cash paid at the time of purchase should be reflected in the worksheet. The remaining installments can be included later as operating expenses in the months in which they're paid.

If the business is leasing the equipment, only upfront lease payments should be included here. The regular monthly lease payments will be included later as a monthly operating expense.

If the business borrowed money for the purchase, you should still forecast the estimated cash payment in the worksheet. The loan will be included later (see the "Startup Cash Received" section on page 44).

| Asset Purchases | Estimated Cost |
|---|---|
| Equipment #1 | $ |
| Equipment #2 | $ |
| Equipment #3 | $ |
| Vehicles | $ |
| Computers | $ |
| Software | $ |
| Printers | $ |
| Telephones | $ |
| Cash Registers | $ |
| Office Furniture | $ |
| Office Equipment | $ |
| Land | $ |
| Buildings | $ |
| Other #1 | $ |
| Other #2 | $ |
| Other #3 | $ |
| **Total Asset Purchases** | $ |

Once you have your asset and equipment purchase estimates, enter your estimates into the Business Forecasting Model.

# Initial Inventory and Raw Material Expenses

To start either a retail or manufacturing business, it will almost always be necessary to purchase inventory or raw materials prior to opening the doors.

If you're starting a retail business, you'll need to buy inventory to stock the store. If you're starting a manufacturing business, you'll need to purchase raw materials so you can begin the production process.

In many cases, as a new business, you'll be required to pay for these purchases at the time of delivery, so you'll need to budget some money to make sure you have the funds for these startup expenses.

In Section 1, you estimated the per-unit cost of this inventory or raw materials. In this section, you should estimate the quantity needed and the total estimated cost of these purchases. You can then enter your estimates into the Business Forecasting Model.

### Initial Production Expenses

| | Cost per Unit | Number of Units | Estimated Cost |
|---|---|---|---|
| **Initial Production Expenses** | | | |
| Raw Material Purchases | $ | | $ |
| Inventory Purchases | $ | | $ |
| Other #1 | $ | | $ |
| Other #2 | $ | | $ |
| **Total Intial Production Expenses** | $ | | $ |

# Other Startup Expenses

In addition to purchasing your equipment and initial inventory and raw materials, you'll incur some other startup expenses. Depending on your business, these expenses might be only a few thousand dollars, or they could be significantly more if the business structure is complex.

The first "other startup expense" a business typically incurs is legal fees. To create a business in any state or province, you typically need to file a series of incorporation documents, which most businesses use a lawyer to prepare. In the worksheet below, use the legal fees line to estimate the how much you'll pay the attorney for these services.

In addition to paying the lawyer, your state, province, and perhaps city will also charge some registration and other fees to process the incorporation papers prepared by the lawyer. These fees should be entered on the state fees line. If your business is also required to pay state, province, or city licensing fees, you should enter these on the license fee line.

Many startups use the services of an accountant or bookkeeper to help set up the business's financial records. If your business has any startup accounting or bookkeeping fees, these should be entered as accounting fees.

Often, a new business owner will take some training classes on writing a business plan or starting a business. The owner or employees may also receive some training on the equipment or software used in the business. If you plan to spend money for your training or the training of your employees, you should enter the estimated amount on the training line.

If your business is renting the space it will use for its operations (such as a store, office or manufacturing facility), and the landlord requires a security deposit or initial rental payments, these fees should be reflected in your startup expense estimates. Likewise, if you're leasing equipment and are required to make upfront security deposit payments, make sure these are entered as well. The security deposits and initial rent payments lines have been provided for this purpose. Finally, the "other lines" can be used for any other startup expenses you expect the business to incur.

Once you've identified and estimated your other startup expenses, enter your estimates into the Business Forecasting Model.

| *Other Startup Expenses* | Estimated Cost |
|---|---|
| Legal Fees | $ |
| State Fees | $ |
| License Fees | $ |
| Accounting Fees | $ |
| Training Expenses | $ |
| Security Deposits | $ |
| Initial Rent Payments | $ |
| Other #1 | $ |
| Other #2 | $ |
| **Total Other Startup Expenses** | $ |

The total startup expenses are the sum of the asset purchases, the initial production expenses, and other startup expenses. Once you've entered the data in the Business Forecasting Model, your total startup expenses will be on the bottom line in the Startup Expenses section of the model.

At minimum, your business will need cash from investors or loans to pay for these startup expenses. The startup cash requirements for the business are discussed in Section 5.

# Sales and Cost of Goods Sold Forecast

 Probably the most important forecast for a business is the projection of sales volume, sales prices and cost of goods sold, but developing an accurate forecast can be a complex process because a typical business will sell a variety of products. Each of these products might have a unique sales price and costs, and the business might sell a different number of each of these products. In this section, we'll discuss how to create these forecasts and how to use the Business Forecasting Model to assist you.

The Business Forecasting Model is set up to allow you to enter the price, cost and sales projections for multiple products. There are four key parts to forecasting sales revenue and cost of goods sold in the Business Forecasting Model:

1. The estimated sales price for each product

2. The estimated cost of acquiring or manufacturing the product that's sold

3. The number of units you expect to sell each month

4. The amount of inventory or raw material the business purchases each month, so products and inventory are available ahead of sales to customers

When you create your sales revenue and costs of goods forecast using the Business Forecasting Model, you'll enter your information into spreadsheets like the ones on page 20. For the rest of this section, we'll provide instructions on how to enter the estimates for each of your products. For every product, you'll be able to estimate average price per sale, costs of goods sold per sale, gross profit per sale, unit sales, inventory and raw materials purchases, and when you pay for your purchases and get paid for your sales.

## Pricing and Cost of Goods Sold

### Product #1
*Enter Product Name Here*

| | |
|---|---|
| Estimated Price per Unit Sale | $ |
| Estimated Cost of Goods per Unit Sale | |
|    Inventory Purchases | $ |
|    Raw Material Purchases | $ |
|    Labor Costs | $ |
| Total COGS per Unit Sale | $ |
| Gross Profit per Unit Sale | $ |
| Gross Margin | 0.0% |

| | Month 0 | Month 1 | Month 2 | Month 3 | Month 4 | Month 5 | Month 6 |
|---|---|---|---|---|---|---|---|
| **Inventory and Raw Material Purchases** | | | | | | | |
| Estimated Units of Inventory or Raw Material Purchased | | | | | | | |
| Number of Days Until Bills are Paid | | | | | | | |
| **Unit Sales** | | | | | | | |
| Estimated Number of Units Sold | | | | | | | |
| Number of Days Until Revenue is Received | | | | | | | |

# Product Name

The Business Forecasting Model allows you to enter sales forecasts for up to six products. If your business offers more than six products, you should either group the similar products or add additional products to the spreadsheets. For each product, enter the name in the "product name" box.

# Average Price per Sale

A good place to start preparing your cash flow projections is by estimating the sales price for your products. In Section 1, we asked you to identify the products and services your business will offer and to estimate the prices you'll charge for these products and services. Once you have these estimates, enter them into the Business Forecasting Model. For each product or service, enter the estimated price per unit sale into the "estimated price per unit sale" cell in the model.

For example, if your business sells coffee and the average sale per customer is $5, you would enter $5 as the estimated price per sale for your coffee products. If your business manufactures and sells office chairs and your chairs sell for $200 each, you would enter $200 as the estimated price per unit sale. If your business sells consulting services and you expect your average rate to be $100 per hour, you would enter $100 as the estimated price per unit sale.

# Cost of Goods Sold per Sale

Once you've estimated the price for each product you sell, you should look at the cost of manufacturing or purchasing the products you sell, or the cost of providing the services you sell.

In Section 1, we also asked you to estimate the cost of purchasing your inventory and raw materials from suppliers. Enter this information into the "inventory purchases" and "raw materials purchases" sections of the Business Forecasting Model.

Additionally, you should enter the direct labor costs associated with producing the products your business is selling. For instance, if you're in the manufacturing business, you'll have labor costs directly associated with the production process (i.e., the wages of the workers on the production line) and labor costs associated with managing the business and running the office.

If your business provides a service, you'll probably have labor costs directly associated with providing this service. This could include the time a consultant spends working on a project for a client, the time an auto mechanic spends repairing a customer's car, or the time a medical professional spends treating patients.

The labor costs of the workers involved in the production of the products or the provision of services should be treated as direct labor costs of the product. Enter these direct labor costs into the "labor costs" section of the Business Forecasting Model.

The labor costs associated with managing the business and running the office are operating expenses. These expenses wouldn't be entered in this spreadsheet;

they will be covered in the "monthly expenses" section of the model (see Section 4 on page 25).

# Gross Profit Per Sale

After you've estimated the price per sale and the cost of goods sold per sale, the Business Forecasting Model will calculate the dollar amount of the gross profit per sale and the gross margin per sale.

Chapter 10 of *Finance Without Fear* contains an extensive discussion of why it's important to understand the margins of your business and how you can obtain data from our website (www.FinanceWithoutFear.com) or industry sources that can be used to compare your business to the industry and your competitors.

In Section 1, we asked that you estimate the margins for your business as well as research the typical margins for your industry. Now that you've estimated your price per sale and your cost of goods sold per sale, you should verify that the gross margin that the model has calculated is consistent with your estimates from Section 1. If your gross margin isn't consistent, either something has changed or is wrong. You should review your estimates and what you input into the model.

# Inventory and Raw Material Purchases

From a cash flow perspective, it's important that you estimate your inventory and raw material purchases.

Before a retail business can open its doors to the public, it must first purchase inventory to stock the shelves of the store. Similarly, a manufacturing business will need to purchase a supply of raw materials before it can produce any products.

For a retail business, it may be necessary to make the initial inventory purchase 15 to 30 days prior to the store opening. It will also be necessary to continue to purchase inventory ahead of sales so the shelves of the store remain stocked.

Manufacturing businesses will also need to make the initial raw material purchases weeks ahead of starting the production process. The time might be reduced to days if a just-in-time inventory process is being used, but the business will also require some raw materials on hand when the production process is running.

Additionally, as you grow a business, you'll need to purchase inventory and raw materials ahead of the sales growth of your business.

The Business Forecasting Model enables you to estimate your raw material and inventory purchases and enter these estimates into the model. At a minimum, we suggest that you estimate some purchases of inventory and raw materials in the month preceding your business opening.

Enter your estimated units of inventory and raw material purchased for each of your products into the appropriate months on the "estimated units of inventory or raw materials purchased" line of the model.

## Payment for Purchases

To develop revenue and cost of goods sold estimates for your business, you must estimate the payment period for each of the products or services your business will purchase.

Chapter 11 in *Finance Without Fear* includes a detailed discussion of the importance of a business's cash payment period. The payment period is the number of days it takes a business to pay for the inventory and raw materials it purchases.

Section 1 included an exercise to evaluate the payment terms that various suppliers will offer to your business. For each of the products offered by your business, you should enter the expected payment terms in the "number of days until bills are paid" line in the model.

## Unit Sales

Once you've estimated how much you'll make on each unit you sell and estimated your inventory purchases, the next step is to estimate how many units you'll sell per month. For example, how many cups of coffee do you expect to sell each month, or office chairs, or hours of consulting?

To accurately project revenue and cost of goods sold expenses, it's very important that you accurately project the number of units the business will sell. Make sure you're realistic about how quickly (or slowly) your sales will grow. Typically, for a startup, sales are slow the first few months, then become more consistent as customers become more aware of the business and begin to make repeat purchases.

It's also important that you include any seasonal adjustments in your sales volume. For instance, for many retail businesses, the bulk of the store's annual sales occur during the Christmas season. A manufacturer supplying merchandise to a retailer for the Christmas season would experience the highest sales volume in late summer as retailers begin to stock up for Christmas. If you sell bathing suits, your sales will be higher in the warm months, and if you sell snow shovels, you can expect your highest sales during the winter months.

The Business Forecasting Model is designed to allow you to forecast your monthly sales volume. The model allows you to input different sales-volume levels for the early months of operation. It also allows you to enter varying sales volumes for different months to account for seasonal fluctuations.

Enter your estimated unit sales for each product into the appropriate months on the "estimated number of units sold" line of the model.

# Payment for Sales

The final section in the spreadsheet covers your collection period. Chapter 11 in *Finance Without Fear* includes a detailed discussion of the importance of a business's collection period. The collection period measures how many days it takes for customers to pay for the goods and services they purchase from a business. The longer it takes customers to pay, the longer the collection period. The longer the collection period, the more working capital the business will need.

Retail stores have a great collection period. Customers either pay cash at the time of purchase, or use a credit card or debit card, where the store gets paid through the bank in a couple of days. At the opposite end are businesses like medical practices or government contractors. These businesses may have to wait six months or more from the time service is rendered to the time they receive cash payment for the service.

Section 1 included an exercise to estimate the cash collection period for each of the products offered by your business. Enter the estimated number of days in the "number of days until revenue is received" section of the model. This information will be used in the calculation of the cash receipts and cash flows of the business.

Once all your estimates for this section have been entered for each product line, the model will estimate the monthly cash flow from selling activities for the business.

For the first few months of a new or growing business, the business may experience a negative cash flow, as it's probably spending more to purchase inventory and raw materials and to manufacture products for sale than it's receiving in revenue from sales. If the monthly cash flow from selling activities doesn't turn positive after the first few months, this isn't a good situation, and the projections should be re-evaluated.

# Monthly Expenses

In addition to startup expenses and the expenses associated with purchasing inventory or manufacturing products, all businesses incur some additional expenses associated with their operations. These additional monthly expenses can be grouped into operating expenses and financing expenses.

Each month, the business will need to use cash to pay these expenses. To create an accurate cash flow forecast, you'll need an accurate cash flow estimate of these expenses.

## Operating Expenses

When you create your monthly operating expenses forecasts, you'll enter the estimates into the "monthly business operating expenses" section of the Business Forecasting Model. An example of this section is shown on page 26.

## Monthly Business Operating Expenses

| | |
|---|---|
| Owners' Salary | $ |
| Employee Salary/Wages | $ |
| Employee Withholding | $ |
| Payroll Expenses | $ |
| Rent | $ |
| Utilities | $ |
| Telephone | $ |
| Internet | $ |
| Equipment Lease Payments | $ |
| Office Supplies | $ |
| Advertising | $ |
| Travel | $ |
| Postage and Delivery | $ |
| Maintenance and Repairs | $ |
| Accounting, Payroll and Legal Services | $ |
| Other Outside Services | $ |
| Insurance | $ |
| Licenses and Fees | $ |
| Income Tax Payments | $ |
| Real Estate and Personal Property Tax | $ |
| Miscellaneous | $ |
| Other | $ |
| **Total Monthly Business Operating Expenses** | **$** |

## Owners' Salary

The first monthly operating expense listed is "owners' salary." Owners' salary is the money the business paid to the owners in salary for the month.

If the owners of the business are actively involved in the operation of the business, they should be receiving a salary. This salary allows the business owners to pay personal bills each month. It also provides an incentive for the owners to remain active in the business. If the owners aren't being paid for participation in the business, there's little incentive to remain active in the company. After all, there are bills to be paid.

Additionally, when an outside investor or lender looks at a business and sees that the owners aren't paying themselves, they aren't likely to invest in the business. A business that can't pay at least a minimal salary to owners who are active in the business isn't a profitable venture.

If the business is profitable, the owners might be able to withdraw their investment from the business or receive dividends from the company. These are discussed in the "Payment to Owners" section on page 36.

## Employee Salary/Wages

Employee salary/wages should include the net amount paid to employees by cash, check, or electronic transfer/direct deposit during the month. This line should include only the cash actually paid to the employees, after the business has withheld payroll taxes, pension or 401(k) payments, and any other employee paid items.

When you're estimating employee's salaries and wages, make sure you don't include any wages you had previously listed as labor costs in cost of goods sold.

## Employee Withholding

The amounts that the business withholds from employees for payroll taxes, pension or 401(k) payments and other employee paid items should be included in employee withholding.

As anyone who has received a paycheck has noticed, the amount of cash you see in your paycheck is substantially different than the amount of money you've earned. For instance, if an employee earns $500 per week, the paycheck received for the week won't be for $500. The gross amount of pay will be $500, but check itself might only be for $400. Why the difference? It's because the employer has withheld estimated income taxes, Social Security and Medicare taxes, and perhaps some other amounts from the paycheck.

By withholding money from employees' paychecks, the employer acts as a tax collection entity for the various government tax collecting agencies. Once the employer has withheld this money, they're required to pay it to various federal, state, and local tax collecting agencies, such as the IRS.

The employer may also withhold other money from an employee's paycheck, such as contributions to a 401(k) or pension plan, health insurance premiums, and even charitable contributions to organizations, such as the United Way.

The "employee withholding" line is used to record the payment of money withheld from an employee's paycheck to the government and other organizations. Note that taxes also must be withheld from the owner's pay. These should be reflected on the employee withholding line as well, as should any withholding from employee wages that have been included as labor costs under costs of goods sold.

It's critical that the employer understand the importance of withholding estimated income taxes and Social Security and Medicare taxes from an employee's paycheck, and the importance of making the required payments to the appropriate government agency on time.

Some startup small-business owners don't realize that withholding taxes from a paycheck is part of their role and hence don't do it, or when cash is tight, they may attempt to evade paying the withholding taxes. This can be a very serious mistake and open the business, and the owners, to serious penalties from the IRS.

## *Payroll Expenses*

In addition to playing a role as tax collector for the IRS and other government agencies, an employer also is responsible for paying certain taxes on behalf of its employees. Specifically, the business is responsible for paying the employer's share of Social Security and Medicare taxes.

As we write this section in mid-2010, the combined Social Security and Medicare tax rates are 15.3 percent of gross employee (or owner) wages. Half this amount (7.65 percent) is deducted from the employee's paycheck as employee withholding, and the employer is responsible for the other 7.65 percent.

The employer's cost for Social Security and Medicare taxes should be included on the "payroll expenses" line. Additionally, payroll expenses can include other taxes, such as unemployment taxes, paid to the state unemployment agency; the employer's share of any health-care premiums; and any employer matches to a 401(k) or pension program.

Like employee withholding expenses, if a business has employees, it will also incur payroll expenses that must be paid. The only exception is if the business is only using the labor of the owner and immediate family members, and nobody is getting a paycheck. In this case, you probably won't have any payroll expenses. In fact, you won't have a payroll. This might occur when the business is first starting or with a family-owned business that isn't yet making money.

## Rent

Beyond payroll expenses, most businesses will incur some expenses associated with their physical location. The first of these expenses is rent.

Most business, particularly those that have just started or that aren't large enough or profitable enough to buy their own building, rent their offices, store, or manufacturing space.

If the business is renting space, the payments should be recorded on the "rent" line. However, if the business is operated out of your home and you don't have a dedicated space that's used solely for your business or you're not paying yourself rent, you should *not* include part of your apartment rental or mortgage payments on your home as expenses. You might be able to deduct some expenses for a home office on your personal income taxes, but if the business isn't paying rent on an actual office or reimbursing you for the use of your home, you shouldn't include part of your personal rent or mortgage payments as operating expenses.

## Utilities

If a business has a physical location outside of your home, it's likely the business will incur some utilities expenses. Utilities expenses include the costs of paying for electricity, gas, oil, water and sewer. In some instances, such as a business located in an office building or a shopping mall, these expenses may be included in the rent the business pays, while in other cases, the business may be responsible for paying the utility bills.

The "utilities" line should be used to estimate the business's payments for utilities. If the business is being operated out of your home, chances are you won't be able to allocate a portion of the household's utility expenses to your business. If the home doesn't have separate utility meters for the rooms in which the business is operated and you can't clearly differentiate the utilities used by the business, the business won't have a utilities expense.

## Telephone

Most businesses have some expenses associated with telephone service. Telephone expenses include the costs of traditional landline and cell phone service for the business.

Although most businesses continue to have their own phone number with a traditional landline service provider, many companies also provide a cell phone to the owner or employees so they can be reached when they're not in the office. In some instances, the business uses *only* a cell phone.

The monthly expenses for business-related phone service should be entered on the "telephone" line. Again, as was the case with utilities, if the business is operated from your home and you don't have a separate phone line for the business, you won't be able to include the costs of the main phone line in your home as a business expense. You'll only be able to include the cost of items that are specifically business related, such as itemized long-distance calls.

## Internet Expenses

Most businesses today use the internet in some way. Almost all businesses have an internet connection that allows the owners and employees to get online to send and receive e-mails and conduct other company business. Many companies also have a company website, which may be used to market the company's products and services, provide information to customers, or conduct e-commerce.

Internet expenses include the costs of providing internet service to your business as well as the costs of hosting your website. This typically includes the cost of providing DSL or cable internet access to your facility and the fees paid to your web-hosting company. It could also include the costs of building and maintaining your website. These costs should be included on the "internet expenses" line.

## Equipment Lease Payments

Many businesses today lease equipment rather than purchasing it outright. Leasing equipment offers businesses certain advantages, such as not needing to make a large cash payment at the time the equipment is acquired and being able to return the equipment at the end of the lease and obtain new equipment with the latest technology.

The cash paid during the month for the use of this equipment should be recorded on the "equipment lease payments" line.

## Office Supplies

The "office supplies" line is where a business would record the purchase of supplies used in the running of the office. Office supplies include items such as pens, paper, and paperclips as well as computer supplies and printer toner, and any custom forms, business cards or letterhead the business uses.

## Advertising

Advertising includes the funds that are spent for advertising your business. This consists of traditional print advertising in newspapers or magazines, online advertising through search engines, as well as the cost of fliers, brochures and trade show exhibits. It also includes paying a design person to create clever advertising materials for you and the cost of designing and operating your website if the purpose of the website is primarily marketing rather than e-commerce.

## Travel

In many businesses, it's necessary for the business owner, salespeople and technical experts to travel to customer meetings and industry events to market their products and to service existing customers.

The business might also own a vehicle, such as a truck, that's used to deliver goods to customers or that the business uses to provide services to customers. An example of the former might be a lumberyard or appliance store that has a fleet of vehicles used to deliver merchandise to construction sites or customers' homes. An example of the latter might be a contractor who uses a business-owned truck to transport equipment to job sites. The expenses for these activities should be entered on the "travel" line.

In many cases, business travel expenses will involve the use of commercial transportation, such as planes, trains, and rental cars or cabs. These are easy to document through the use of receipts and should be included on the travel line.

Less easy to document is use of the owner's or an employee's personal vehicle in business travel. If a personal vehicle is used, the business should be very strict about recording how many miles were driven for business purposes and how many were driven for personal reasons. This becomes important for two reasons: 1) You need to know what you're actually spending on transportation in the business, and 2) the IRS won't allow you to deduct all expenses for the vehicle if you use it part of the time for personal reasons.

## Postage and Delivery

Postage and delivery includes the costs the business pays to third parties to deliver its goods to customers and to mail items using the postal service.

For a retailer, this might include the costs of shipping merchandise purchased online from the store or warehouse to the customer's home. For a manufacturer, this might include the freight charges incurred to ship merchandise from the factory to the retailer. For a service business, this might include the costs of shipping documents and reports to the customer, using a delivery service such as UPS or FedEx.

## Maintenance and Repairs

Maintenance and repairs should include the cost of any repairs or maintenance done and paid for on buildings or equipment the business owns.

Remember that this is a cash flow statement, so you shouldn't be setting aside money for future repairs on this line. Reserves (discussed on page 38) are where a business can set aside money for prospective future repairs.

## Accounting, Payroll and Legal Expenses

Payments your business makes to accountants, bookkeepers, a payroll service, attorneys and other professional service providers should be recorded on the "accounting, payroll and legal expenses" line.

These might include expenses paid to your attorney for incorporating the business or setting it up as a limited liability corporation. They might also include the costs of having your initial financial statements set up by a bookkeeper or accountant. On an ongoing basis, these might include the costs of paying a bookkeeper to record your monthly transactions and maintain your books, and the annual costs of having an accountant prepare your financial statements and perhaps perform an audit.

Maintaining payroll records can be one of the most tedious and time-consuming tasks a business has to perform. Not only is it necessary to keep track of the wage or salary rates and withholding amounts for all employees, but state and federal withholding tax tables are continually updated as laws and regulations change. For this reason, many businesses use a payroll services company, such as ADP or Paychex, to manage their payroll. Others use a payroll service that's integrated into an accounting package, such as QuickBooks. Using a payroll service allows businesses to focus on making money through operations.

The cost of payroll services should be included on the "accounting, payroll and legal services" line.

## Other Outside Services

Other outside services would include payments made to consultants, architects, software developers, and other outside expertise you need to run your business.

When a business uses outside services, it should always document the relationship between the service provider and the business through the use of a written contract.

A key issue a company faces in using an outside contractor to provide a service is that the service provider must be truly independent from the business. The business can specify the services to be provided but not control the contractor in the provision of those services. If the business exerts too much control, the IRS may deem the outside contractor to be an employee rather than an independent contractor.

To protect against this event, payments should be made to the outside contractor's business rather than to an individual and should document the relationship in a written contract.

It's beyond the scope of this book to fully explain this aspect of employment law. Suffice it to say that how an outside contractor is hired and controlled is critical. State labor departments periodically investigate these relationships, even in small businesses. A business should rely on an attorney for advice in these matters.

## Insurance

The "insurance" line is used to record the insurance-related expenses of the business. Any payments for insurance necessitated by the business should be estimated here. This might include insurance for liability, workers' compensation, inventory and vehicles.

Insurance provided to employees, such as health insurance, should be included as a payroll expense; this was discussed on page 28.

## Licenses and Fees

Some businesses incur periodic costs for licenses and fees, which are typically paid to a city or state agency. For example, many professions, ranging from barbers and contractors through attorneys and doctors, are required to have a license to practice in their state. The cost of these licenses is often paid by the business and should be recorded on the licenses and fees line.

Additionally, the business may be required to pay a variety of fees to city or state agencies as part of the regulatory process. For instance, the secretary of state's office or county clerk's office may require a fee be paid by a company for such activities as processing the business's incorporation papers, changing the business's name or address, or processing notification of changes in the business's officers. These expenses would be recorded on the "licenses and fees" line.

## Income Tax Payments

The good news is you've created and are maintaining a profitable business. The bad news is, since your business is profitable, the federal government, probably your state government and perhaps your city government, want a percentage of your profits in the form of taxes. The "income tax payments" line is used to record the income tax payments to be made to the federal, state and local governments.

Earlier we discussed the role a business played in withholding income tax payments from employee wages and salaries. The business withholds some money from each paycheck for taxes and pays this money to the appropriate government agency. The government uses this process to collect money from employees as the money is earned. The government gets the money up front and doesn't have to worry about the employee saving money for a large payment at the end of the year.

Business income tax payments work much the same way. The government taxing agencies require that businesses make quarterly estimated income tax payments throughout the year based on their estimated profits, and then make a final payment once the final profits for the year are known.

For most small businesses, the accountant or bookkeeper helps the business owner prepare these profit estimates and estimated tax payments. In larger businesses, the comptroller or treasurer's department is responsible for preparing estimated tax payments.

### Real Estate and Personal Property Taxes

In addition to paying income taxes, a business may also be required to pay taxes on the real estate and other property it owns.

If the business is renting its offices, there's no need to worry about real estate taxes, because they're the responsibility of the property owner. However, if the business owns any of its business locations, real estate taxes are the responsibility of the business. These taxes should be recorded on the "real estate and personal property taxes" line.

Additionally, many states have taxes on personal property. As applied to businesses, personal property is often defined as the machinery and equipment the business owns, including computers. The state or local taxing agency levies a tax on the value of these assets. When paid by the business, these taxes should also be recorded on the "real estate and personal property taxes" line.

If you're running a small business from your home, and you're able to clearly delineate the business use of the property from your personal use, you may be able to pay a percentage of the property taxes on your home from the business. If you chose to do this, consult with your accountant first to make sure you don't run afoul of tax regulations.

### Miscellaneous

Miscellaneous expenses might be small expenses that haven't been specifically broken out as operating expenses. Miscellaneous expenses might also be one-time expenses the business incurs that are not expected to be recurring expenses.

### *Other*

The "other" expenses line should be used for any other operating expenses that haven't been included above.

The miscellaneous and other categories are vague, and vague categories on financial statements are sure to raise questions. Businesses should try to keep entries in these categories to a minimum. If the amounts in the miscellaneous and other categories become too large, it's a good idea to identify the specific expenses and add them as line items to the "monthly business operating expenses" section of the Business Forecasting Model.

Once you've entered all your monthly operating expenses into the Business Forecasting Model, the model will calculate the total operating expenses for the month.

# Financing Activities

In addition to the monthly operating expenses, a business might also have monthly payments associated with financing activities.

Monthly payments for financing activities include payments on loans, payments a business makes to the owners, and payments a business makes into reserve and escrow accounts.

### *Payments on Loans*

If a business borrows money, it will be required to make periodic interest and loan payments. Loan payments are entered into the "Payments on Loans" worksheet in the "monthly expenses" section of the Business Forecasting Model. (An example of this worksheet is below.)

---

**Payments on Loans**

| | |
|---|---|
| Interest Payments on Loans | $ |
| Principal Payments on Loans | $ |
| **Total Loan Payments** | $ |

---

## Interest Payments on Loans

If the business has borrowed money from a lender, such as a bank, credit union, community loan fund, or on a credit card, the lender will charge the business interest on those loans. For example, if you made a payment on business's credit card of $1,000, and $950 of that was used to pay off the principal portion of the bill, and $50 was for the interest you're paying, you should put the $50 on this line.

The payment of the interest on the loans during the month should be included on the "interest payments on loans" line.

## Principal Payments on Loans

If the business has borrowed money from a lender, in addition to charging interest, the lender at some point will expect the principal balance on the loan to be repaid.

The lender may require the business to pay some principal each month, let the business defer payment of principal until some point in the future and then require a lump-sum "balloon" payment, or allow the business to make principal payments as the cash flow of the business allows. For example, if you made a payment on the business's credit card for $1,000, and $950 of that was to pay off the principal portion of the bill, and $50 was for the interest you're paying, you should put the $950 on this line.

The payment of principal on the loans during the month should be recorded on the "principal payments on loans" line.

Principal payments on loans and interest payments on loans can either be entered here as financing expenses, or they can be entered as a source of startup cash for the business in Section 5. If the information on the loan is entered as discussed in Section 5, the applicable payment amounts will flow to the cash flow projections, and you don't need to make any entries here.

## *Payments to Owners*

In addition to paying back its lenders, a business might also make payments to return the owners' investment or to pay profits to the owners. Payments to owners are entered into the "monthly expenses" section of the Business Forecasting Model. (An example of the "Payments to Owners" worksheet is on page 37.)

---

### *Payments to Owners*

| | |
|---|---|
| Withdrawal of Owners' Investment | $ _____ |
| Equity Investors' Withdrawals | $ _____ |
| Dividend Payments | $ _____ |
| **Total Payments to Owners** | **$** _____ |

---

## Withdrawal of Owners' Investment

The "withdrawal of owners' investment" line should be used to record the cash that's paid to an owner of the business when that owner withdraws funds that have been invested in the company.

This line should include only the withdrawal of cash the owner has previously invested in the business. These investments would previously have been recorded as an owners' investment. Any salary paid to the owner should be reflected on the owners' salary line (discussed previously on page 26), and any profits withdrawn should be reflected as dividend payments (discussed below).

It's very common for this line to show a zero in the early days of any startup business, as the owners' money is used to pay startup expenses and grow the company. In general, the business owner shouldn't withdraw his/her initial investments until the business is profitable and other equity investors have been paid.

## Equity Investors' Withdrawals

The equity investors' withdrawals line should be used to record the cash that's paid to the business's equity investors when they withdraw funds that have been invested in the company.

As is the case with the withdrawal of owners' investment, equity investors' withdrawals should only record the repayment of the equity investors' original investment. The payment of profits to the equity investors should be reflected as dividend payments, which are discussed below.

## Dividend Payments

The "dividend payments" line should be used to record the payment of dividends or profits to both the owners and equity investors.

When a business is profitable, it's time to pay all or a percentage of the profits to those who invested in the business. A business uses dividends to pay profits to its investors.

In many small businesses, it's possible for the owners to both receive a salary if they're actively involved in business operations and to receive a share of the profits in the form of dividends.

## Reserves

Reserves are amounts of cash the business has set aside for emergencies or other expenditures that you know you'll have in the near future. Reserves are entered into the "Other Payments" worksheet in the "monthly expenses" section of the Business Forecasting Model. (An example of this worksheet is found below.)

| Other Payments | |
|---|---|
| Reserves | $ |
| **Total Other Payments** | $ |

Typically, reserves are held in a separate bank account from the business's other cash so the money isn't inadvertently used for operations.

If a business knows that a certain key piece of equipment needs to be replaced in the near future, it might begin saving cash in the reserves bank account so the funds are available when the time comes to purchase the new machine.

Another example of use of the "reserves" line might be a seasonal business, such as a Christmas specialty store. A Christmas specialty store will make most of its sales in the two-month period leading up to Christmas, yet it will incur operating expenses year round. A profitable Christmas specialty store will save most of its profits from the Christmas season in reserves so the business has enough cash to operate during the off-season.

Once the monthly business operating expenses, payments on loans, payments to owners, and reserve payments have been entered into the Business Forecasting Model, the model will automatically calculate the total monthly expenses payments.

# How Much Cash Do You Need?

Now that you've entered the revenue and expenses information for your business, let's look at your cash flow and see how much the business needs to pay in startup expenses, costs of goods expenses, and monthly expenses until sufficient revenue from sales begins coming in.

Let's start by looking at the money needed to pay the business' startup expenses. At a minimum, you'll need sufficient cash to pay your startup expenses. In Section 2, you projected your startup expenses. Startup expenses include the money you expect to spend on asset purchases, to make your initial purchases of inventory and raw materials, and to pay the other expenses of starting the business.

## Sources of Startup Cash

There are three basic sources of startup cash for a business:

- Money you or your friends and family invest
- Money the business borrows from a bank or other lender
- Money that outside investors and venture capitalists invest

Let's look at each of these sources individually, and for a more detailed discussion on finding the money to start and operate your business, read Chapter 21 in *Finance Without Fear*.

## *Your Money*

In almost all instances, the owner's own money is the initial source of capital for a new business. If possible, it's best that you start your business using entirely your own funds. This is because you don't have to spend time explaining to others how the business is going to make money and how you intend to repay them. *You* need to understand how the business is going to make money, but it won't be necessary to create lots of documentation to explain it to others.

Typically, an owner's own money comes either from savings, retirement accounts, the equity he/she has in their house or personal credit cards.

Your savings accounts are easiest to access and should be looked at first. You could use retirement funds, but these funds are often only available to you with taxes to be paid and early withdrawal penalties. And, of course, you're depleting the money you need for your retirement.

You could turn to the equity in your home through a mortgage refinancing, home equity loan or line of credit. These loans tend to have relatively low interest rates but carry a risk of losing the home if the loan can't be repaid.

Credit cards are a very common source of startup funding but generally carry high interest rates and tricky provisions that can make them a very expensive way to borrow. However, many startup businesses have been funded using cash advances from the owner's credit cards.

Use the "Personal Funds" worksheet below to identify how much of your own money you have available to invest in the business.

---

### *Personal Funds*

| | |
|---|---|
| Savings | $ _____ |
| Retirement Funds | $ _____ |
| Home Equity | $ _____ |
| Credit Card #1 | $ _____ |
| Credit Card #2 | $ _____ |
| Credit Card #3 | $ _____ |
| Other | $ _____ |
| **Total** | $ _____ |

---

## *Family and Friends*

The second best option for funding your startup business is to turn to your family and friends. One of the advantages of obtaining startup financing from family and friends is that they understand your work ethic and are often willing to invest in your business based on this and the strength of your character, without forcing you through the same underwriting process a professional lender would use.

If the business doesn't go as expected, family members are likely to be the most understanding or forgiving of an extended payback because they'll have strong ties to you beyond the loan they gave you. Of course, if things go poorly, you run the risk of having family members who will never talk to you again because your business failed, and you didn't pay them back.

Friends are the next best source of funding and have some of the same positives as family members. Friends are likely to be somewhat understanding if things go badly and your payback becomes extended. However, as with family members, you're at the risk of losing a friend if the money they lend you is lost, and you're never able to pay them back.

As the business owner, you should make sure that the lender (your family and friends) fully understands the risk of their loan or investment. If not, you risk that your lender or investor will suddenly wake up and demand payment, which could be very disruptive for the business.

In the "Money from Family and Friends" worksheet below, list the money family and friends will invest in the business.

---

### *Money from Family and Friends*

| | |
|---|---|
| Family Member Investment #1 | $ |
| Family Member Investment #2 | $ |
| Investment by Friends #1 | $ |
| Investment by Friends #2 | $ |
| **Total** | **$** |

## Loans

Your own money and the investment from your family and friends may not be enough to fully fund your business startup. When this happens, you'll need to look to a small-business lender or investor for the additional money.

The next most likely source of funds is a loan from a lending institution. Typical small-business lenders include banks and credit unions as well as community loan funds. You might also be able to get a loan from a lender who issues Small Business Administration (SBA) loans.

To obtain a loan, you'll need to prepare financial projections and a business plan that demonstrate that the business will have sufficient cash flow to repay the loan. (For a detailed discussion of how lenders evaluate a business when making lending decisions, read Chapter 21 in *Finance Without Fear*.)

Use the "Money Obtained from Loans" worksheet below to list the sources and amount of loans the business will acquire. You should also list the terms of the loan, such as the interest rate and term, as these are needed to calculate the monthly loan payment.

### Money Obtained from Loans

| | Amount | Interest Rate | Term |
|---|---|---|---|
| Bank Loan #1 | $ | % | |
| Bank Loan #2 | $ | % | |
| SBA Loan | $ | % | |
| Community Loan Fund | $ | % | |
| Other #1 | $ | % | |
| Other #2 | $ | % | |
| **Total** | $ | | |

## Outside Investors and Venture Capitalists

The final source of startup investment for a business are outside investors and venture capitalists.

An outside investor is any unrelated person or organization that invests in your business. Outside investors include wealthy individuals in your community who invest in new ventures as a sideline, or professionals who make a living investing in businesses for themselves or on behalf of their clients, or any-where in between.

Venture capitalists are a special type of outside investor who specialize in providing startup and growth financing to businesses with exceptional growth potential. Venture capitalists are very common in the computer and software industry as well as in certain parts of the pharmaceutical and medical fields.

Obtaining startup capital from outside investors and venture capitalists is not only very difficult, but you'll find that these types of investors aren't as warm and cuddly as lenders from banks, credit unions or community loan funds.

Outside investors and venture capitalists invest in businesses with the expectation of making a return on their investments for themselves and their clients. Typically, an investment from an outside investor or venture capitalist is made in the form of an equity investment rather than a loan. This means that when outside investors or venture capitalists invest in your business, they receive an ownership interest in the business. That is, they own a piece of your business. Depending on the amount of money they provide and the terms you negotiate, they may own a small percentge of the business, or a large percentage.

On the "Money from Outside Investors and Venture Capitalists" worksheet below, list any investments the business will receive from venture capitalists and other outside investors.

---

### Money from Outside Investors and Venture Capitalists

| Source | Amount | Terms and Conditions |
|---|---|---|
| Outside Investor #1 | $ | |
| Outside Investor #2 | $ | |
| Venture Capitalist #1 | $ | |
| Venture Capitalist #2 | $ | |
| **Total** | $ | |

---

Once you've identified the sources of startup cash for your business, enter these into the startup cash inflows section (see page 44) of the Business Forecasting Model.

### Startup Cash Received

**Startup Cash Received**

*Enter Company Name Here*

| Equity Investment | Amount |
|---|---|
| Owners' Investment #1 | $ |
| Owners' Investment #2 | $ |
| Owners' Investment #3 | $ |
| Owners' Investment #4 | $ |
| Investment by Family | $ |
| Investment by Friends | $ |
| Outside Investors | $ |
| Venture Capital Investment | $ |
| **Total Equity Investment** | $ |

| Loans | Amount | Interest Rate | Term | Balloon or Amortizing? |
|---|---|---|---|---|
| Bank Loan #1 | $ | % | | |
| Bank Loan #2 | $ | % | | |
| SBA Loan | $ | % | | |
| Community Loan Fund | $ | % | | |
| Other #1 | $ | % | | |
| Other #2 | $ | % | | |
| **Total Loans** | $ | | | |
| **Total Startup Cash Received** | $ | | | |

# Projected Cash Flows

After the startup cash inflows have been entered, the Business Forecasting Model has all the information necessary to project the cash flows for the business.

In the "financial projections" section in the Business Forecasting Model are the estimated cash flows for your business for the first three years of operations. The estimated cash flows show:

- Cash the business has at the beginning of each period
- Cash inflows to the business during the period
- Cash outflows from the business during the period
- Cash the business has at the end of the period

The "Projected Cash Flow Table" below is an example of how projected cash flows might look for a startup business in the Business Forecasting Model.

| *Projected Cash Flow* | Month 1 | Month 2 | Month 3 |
|---|---|---|---|
| **Cash Received** | | | |
| Equity Investment | $45,000 | | |
| Loans | $65,000 | | |
| Revenue | $0 | $0 | $12,500 |
| **Total Cash Received** | **$110,000** | **$0** | **$12,500** |
| **Cash Paid** | | | |
| Startup Expenses | | | |
| Asset Purchases | $40,000 | | |
| Initial Production Expenses | $10,000 | | |
| Other Startup Expenses | $1,000 | | |
| Cost of Inventory and Materials | $0 | $9,000 | $9,000 |
| Operating Expenses | $8,100 | $11,100 | $14,100 |
| Payments on Loans | | | |
| Interest Payments | $625 | $619 | $613 |
| Principal Payments | $612 | $618 | $625 |
| Payments to Owners | | | |
| Other Payments | $0 | $0 | $0 |
| **Total Cash Paid** | **$60,337** | **$21,337** | **$24,338** |
| **Net Cash Flow** | **$49,663** | **($21,337)** | **($11,838)** |
| **Beginning of Period Cash** | $0 | $49,663 | $28,326 |
| Plus Net Cash Flow | $49,663 | ($21,337) | ($11,838) |
| **End of Period Cash** | **$49,663** | **$28,326** | **$16,488** |

## Beginning of Period Cash

The cash the business has at the beginning of the period should be zero for the first month of the business. That is, the business starts with no money on its first day, then begins to receive money from its owners and spends money to pay its bills.

For each following month, the cash the business has at the beginning of the month should be the same as the cash it has at the end of the prior month.

## Cash Received

The "cash received" section of the "Projected Cash Flow" worksheet (on page 45) includes any startup cash flowing into the business, such as the owners' investment, or money received from a bank loan or during the month from selling products and services.

During the first month of operation, there should be startup cash inflows into the business, although that money may or may not come from the sale of its products or services. When the business gets paid for its products and services depends on its collection period. Recall that when you projected the sales of the business's products and services, you were also asked to project the collection period for the business.

The Business Forecasting Model uses the collection period you entered in the sales and cost of goods sold section to align the cash received from customers in the model with the timing of its expected receipt by the business.

For instance, if you indicated that it takes 30 days for customers to pay for purchases, the model will lag the payments from customers by 30 days. In other words, the cash from a customer who makes a purchase in January will be received in February.

Similarly, if you indicated the business had a long collection period, such as the 180 days it might take a medical practice or government contractor to get paid, the model will adjust the cash receipts from sales so that payment for services provided in January will be received in July.

## Cash Paid

The "cash paid" section of the "Projected Cash Flow" worksheet includes any cash the business has spent on startup expenses, cost of goods sold, and the business's monthly expenses. (For detailed descriptions of business startup expenses, costs of goods sold expenses, and a business's monthly expenses, refer to Sections 2, 3 and 4, respectively.)

As was the case with the Business Forecasting Model lagging the receipt of cash payments from customers to reflect the collection period, the Business

Forecasting Model will lag the payment of cost of goods sold expenses to reflect the payment period of the business.

That is, if the business purchases inventory or raw materials, and there's a lag between when the purchases are made and when payment is due, the model will adjust the cash outflows to account for this payment period. For a business that purchases inventory in January, with a 60-day payment period, the cash payments for these purchases will be reflected in the cash flow forecast as occurring in March.

### End of Period Cash

The total of the cash received for the period, less the cash paid, is the net cash flow for the period. A positive number indicates that the business took in more cash than it spent during the period. A negative number indicates that the business spent more cash than it took in during the period.

At the end of each month, the Business Forecasting Model will calculate the end of period cash position. The end of period cash is the beginning of period cash position, plus the net cash flow.

If the net cash flow is positive, the business will have more cash at the end of the month than it started with. If the net cash flow is negative, the business will have less cash at the end of the month than it started with.

When you're forecasting the operation of your business, you should be very concerned if the end of period cash is negative because this means the business doesn't have enough cash to pay all its bills. If your business has a negative end of period cash position at the end of any month, the business will need additional loans or investment by the owners or other investors.

In general, negative cash flows during the early months of a business are nothing to worry about, provided the business begins to show a positive net cash flow in later months. However, if your business is generating a negative net cash flow every month, you should re-examine your assumptions. Either your assumptions are wrong, or the business may not be profitable.

## Additional Cash Needs

We started this section by noting that at a minimum, a business needs sufficient cash to pay its startup expenses. In fact, a startup business often needs additional cash (beyond what's used to pay startup expenses) to cover monthly expenses until the business is generating sufficient cash flows from the sales of its products and services.

To determine if your business will need additional cash to fund startup operations, examine the end of period cash number on the projected cash flow table. If the end of period cash is negative in one or more months, the business will need additional startup cash before it begins operations—enough to cover its largest cash deficit.

You should identify additional sources of startup cash and enter this information into the startup "cash inflows" section of the Business Forecasting Model. Once you've done so and made the entries in the model, you should re-examine the end of period cash positions for each month in the "Projected Cash Flow" worksheet. The business should no longer have a cash deficit in any month.

# Sensitivity Analysis

 The last step in forecasting the financial operations of your business is to examine the sensitivity of your business to changes in one or more of your estimates. That is, you want to find out what will happen to the cash flow and financial projections of your business if there's a variance in some of the key estimates.

As you may have noticed as you read the prior sections of this workbook and gathered your data to input into the Business Forecasting Model, the cash flows of the business are very dependent on the profit margin made from each sale, the level of sales achieved, and how quickly the business is able to build its sales volume. If your estimates for any of these aren't correct, your cash flow, cash needs, and profitability projections may not be correct, either.

The key to making money from your business is to sell your products and services at a price that will allow you to pay all the expenses of the business, with some money left over as profit. You must also have enough cash available to offset any timing differences between when your customers pay you and when you must pay your bills.

To accomplish these goals, it's very important that you understand the sensitivity of your business's cash flows to changes in prices, cost of goods sold, number of units sold, and operating expenses.

## Revenue

A key question facing many business owners is what happens to profitability if they aren't able to obtain the sales revenue they estimated for their business's goods and services. Examining the cash flows and profits of your business under different pricing scenarios may provide the answers.

There are several reasons your revenue projections could vary from your initial estimates: You obtain a different product mix than you estimated, you're selling your products and services for a higher or lower price than you estimated, or you periodically put your products "on sale."

## Product Mix

If your business sells multiple products, you'll have estimated a price and number of units sold for each product you sell, but if you don't sell exactly this combination of products, your sales and your cash flow will be different. In your sensitivity analysis, you might estimate different combinations of the product mix to see the effect on your cash flow projections.

For example, if your business sold two products—one for $10 and the other for $30—and you expected to sell the same number of units of each, your average sale price would be $20. However, if you sold twice as many $10 products as you did $30 products, your average sale price would be only $16.67, not $20, and your total cash flow from sales would be less.

## Lower Prices

You might also examine the effect a lower unit price would have on your cash flow projections. A lower unit price might occur if you've overestimated the price your customers are willing to pay for your products or services, and you find yourself having to lower your prices.

For example, if you estimated that the average customer in your restaurant would pay $25 for dinner, you could examine the effect on your cash flow projections if the average customer purchased your less expensive meals so that your average revenue per meal was only $20. You could also examine your financial projections if the average meal was $30.

## Sale Prices

A lower unit price might also occur if you periodically offer your merchandise at sale prices. Many retail businesses either hold periodic sales to attract customers to the store, or discount seasonal or discontinued merchandise to free up space in the store. You should examine the sensitivity of your cash flow projections when the business receives a lower per unit price as a result of placing merchandise on sale.

# Cost of Goods Sold

Another key variable to your cash flow projections is the cost of goods sold. If the cost of purchasing inventory is higher than your estimates, or the cost of the raw materials or labor used in the production of your products is higher than your estimates, and you're not able to pass these cost increases onto your customers in the form of higher prices, the gross margin and gross profits of your business will be lower.

As part of your sensitivity analysis, you should examine the effect that increases in cost of goods sold could have on your cash flows. For example, if the revenue per meal in your restaurant is $25 and the cost of producing this meal is $20, the business makes a gross profit of $5 for each meal served. However, if there's a drought this year and the price of food increases, the cost of producing each meal might increase to $22, reducing the gross profit per meal to $3. If this happens, will the business still generate enough cash to pay its bills?

# Unit Sales

One of the primary assumptions used in forecasting the cash flows for your business is the number of units of each product or service that will sell each month. For that reason, your sensitivity analysis might examine the cash flow projections of the business at different levels of sales.

For example, if you expected your restaurant to sell 1,000 meals a month, you might analyze your financial projections and assume the business sold 1,100 meals per month or 900 meals per month. If fewer meals are sold, does the business still have sufficient cash flow to pay all its expenses?

One of the principal uses of sensitivity analysis for a startup business is to examine how quickly or slowly sales volume builds. When you project the unit sales for your business in the Business Forecasting Model, it allows you to project different sales for startup and seasonal periods.

Based on these unit sale projections, the model projects the cash flows for the business. You can then use these cash flow projections to estimate the amount of startup cash the business will need.

Clearly, how quickly you assume the sales volume will grow is a key assumption. As part of the sensitivity analysis for your business, you should vary the speed at which the sales volume grows.

Again using the example of the restaurant, if you projected the number of meals sold to grow to 1,000 per month by the end of the third month, you should examine the cash flow projections if the number of meals sold grows more slowly. What happens to the cash flows and startup cash needs of the business if the sales volume doesn't reach 1,000 meals per month until the fourth month? Or until the fifth month, or the sixth month? What happens if sales never reach 1,000 meals per month? Will the business still generate enough cash to survive?

Also, because businesses must purchase inventory and raw materials for the production process ahead of sales, and because there are timing differences between when payment for sales are received and when payment for inventory and raw materials must be made, you should analyze the sensitivity of the business to sales growing faster than planned. Faster sales growth might also have a negative effect on the cash flow projections of the business when there's a significant difference between the collection period and the payment period. A great example of this is a medical practice. In a typical medical practice, reimbursement for patient treatments may not be received for six months or more after service is rendered. If the business plans on providing 500 treatments per month and suddenly finds itself giving 600 per month, it may find itself in a cash crisis since it will be spending money to provide these additional treatments but won't be collecting payment for six months.

## Operating Expenses

Finally, you might want to analyze the sensitivity of the cash flow projections to changes in operating expenses.

When you prepared your initial operating expense projections for your business, you may have known the exact amount for some of the monthly operating expenses, but you may have estimated the monthly amount for some of the other costs. You might consider varying the amount of some of the estimated expenses and analyzing the impact these changes have on the cash flow projections of the business, particularly the startup cash needed.

## Congratulations!

Once you've completed these steps, you will have successfully forecasted the cash flows, cash needs, and financial operations of your business.

If the projected net cash flows of your business are positive after a few months of operations and remain so throughout the various scenarios of your sensitivity analysis, you will have succeeded in designing a profitable business.

It's time to move forward with the creation of your business.

# Accessing the Business Forecasting Model Website and Spreadsheet Directions

 The Business Forecasting Model is based on Excel spreadsheets and is comprised of several worksheet sections, spreadsheets and charts. The model is designed to allow you to develop cash flow forecasts and financial projections for your business. Your role is to research your business, develop the assumptions and estimates for your business, and then enter these estimates (as described in the workbook) into the appropriate sections of the Business Forecasting Model.

The Business Forecasting Model is available to all registered owners of this workbook. It can be downloaded from our website at www.FinanceWithoutFear.com.

To get the most out of the Business Forecasting Model, you should:

- Have Microsoft Excel version 2003 or later loaded on your computer
- Have a basic understanding of Excel and how to use it
- Know how to download a file from our website and save it on your computer's hard drive

Note that although the printed tables in this workbook are taken from the spreadsheet model, to get the most out of this workbook and the Business Forecasting Model, you should download the model and work through it as you read the sections in the workbook.

# Downloading the Business Forecasting Model

1. Open your web browser (Internet Explorer, Firefox, Safari, etc.).

2. Go to our website www.FinanceWithoutFear.com.

3. Click on the link for the Business Forecasting Model. (This should bring you to the link for the Business Forecasting Model: www.financewithoutfear.com/businessforecastingmodel)

4. To access the model and download the spreadsheet, you must register. The registration process is brief. Follow the registration instructions on the screen. During the registration process, you'll be asked for a Business Forecasting Model registration code. The registration code for owners of this workbook is: **bfmworkbook2011**.

5. If you've already registered, sign in using your e-mail address and password.

6. Once you're registered and signed in, you'll be able to download the Business Forecasting Model and sample company spreadsheets for the three sample companies used in *Finance Without Fear*. At this point, you should see a series of files:

- **The Business Forecasting Model for Excel 2007 or higher users:**
  Business_Forecasting_Model.xlsx

- **The Business Forecasting Model for Excel 2003 users:**
  Business_Forecasting_Model.xls

- **Bonnie's Beachwear Startup for Excel 2007 or higher users:**
  Bonnies_Beachwear_Startup.xlsx

- **Bonnie's Beachwear Startup for Excel 2003:**
  Bonnies_Beachwear_Startup.xls

- **Boutique Handbag Startup for Excel 2007 or higher users:**
  Boutique_Handbag_Startup.xlsx

- **Boutique Handbag Startup for Excel 2003:**
  Boutique_Handbag_Startup.xls

- **Uptown Chiropractic Startup for Excel 2007 or higher users:**
  Uptown_Chiropractic_Startup.xlsx

- **Uptown Chiropractic Startup for Excel 2003:**
  Uptown_Chiropractic_Startup.xls

7. Click on Excel file "Business_Forecasting_Model.xlsx" or "Business_Forecasting_Model.xls."

8. Your browser should ask you if you want to open the file or save it. Choose save, and save it to a folder on your computer.

9. You can now leave your web browser.

10. Go to the folder where you saved the "Business_Forecasting_Model.xlsx" or "Business_Forecasting_Model.xls" Excel workbook file and open it.

*If you have any difficulty registering, please contact us at:*
*register@financewithoutfear.com.*

# Index

*Bill dedicates this book to his wife, Ann-Marie.*
*Thanks for being there as I worked on this book.*
*Your input is more valuable than you will ever know.*

*John dedicates this book to his wife, Eileen.*
*You are the best thing that ever happened to me.*
*You make me want to be a better man.*